My Life Tested

EARTHLY VS. SPIRITUAL THINGS

By Theresa M. Odom-Surgick

Published by:

FriesenPress

Suite 300 — 852 Fort Street
Victoria, BC, Canada V8W 1H8

www.friesenpress.com

Distributed to the trade by The Ingram Book Company

TABLE OF CONTENTS

Dedicated to the memory of my mom
Delila Melrose Jacobs-Odom

For the example of love, wisdom and strength that are shown
and expressed through my Daddy, Benjamin Odom

To my husband, Arnold for his love and devotion
To my beloved children ~ Shawne, Andrae, Antoine &
Krystal-Rose
And adopted children, Christopher & Shayla Armand

Also to my siblings ~ Denise, Rose and Benjamin Alexander Odom
And my God Sister, Cheryl Royal

With all of my love to each of you!

FOREWORD

Something incredible has happened. God has shown His awesomeness once again and continues to outdo Himself as He let His light shine in one of His own — my friend Theresa.

To everything, there is a season. I believe that it was in the mid-eighties when we met at a church function- I was a graduate student at a local college visiting one of many churches in the area and she was the church's gospel choir director. Having grown up in the church and longing to join in somewhere to have a home away from home (with some "real" church folk), I joined the church where Theresa was an active, dedicated and sincere servant in Christ. Her beautiful spirit was one where you could readily see His beauty and grace in her as she worked tirelessly in ministering to others and spreading Christ's liberating gospel through music, word and deed.

She was quite shy when speaking to others one-on-one, but when doing so it was easy to ascertain that God was using her quiet and humble spirit to spread His word and receive His calling. As a result, I too became an active "visiting" member of the same church where I continued to work for a couple of years until I graduated and moved away. During my time there, Theresa and I became close friends. What an honor and a privilege it was to share that season and wonderful time in my life with such a wonderful Christian woman.

As a tight knit family person — wife and mother of three (she then since added another), I watched her work in amazement as she seemingly made time for her husband, kids, church choir, gospel music group and full-time job working nonstop. She let Christ's light shine through her tireless efforts to grow in His word and work in all aspects of her life. Endlessly, Theresa demonstrated her faith through work in the church, at home and on her job. Her commitment to Christ was evident and I honestly never heard her complain.

Now, she has decided to continue to humbly seek His grace and mercy through her own eyes and on paper for others to see. Without judgment and through much prayer, I witnessed her sharing opened wounds, trials and tribulations over time but once again, God showed up. This time, this season, for whatever reason, He used her to share her humanness to serve as a witness to others letting them know that no matter what you're going through, God may still use you to let His light shine and He still carries you and will never give up on you. Still friends today, I am honored to be a part of this personal journey with Theresa and I wish her nothing short of God's blessings as she continues on His battlefield — a quiet, meek, humble, sincere and Christ filled servant.

To God, be the glory for the things He continues to do.

Regards,

Natalie C. Johnson

INTRODUCTION

Several years ago, I had an opportunity to sit down and watch the Bobby Jones Gospel Program on BET Television. That night they were televising the "Vision Awards". These awards were being given to people who had made outstanding achievements in the Gospel music field. One of the recipients of an award came to the podium and proceeded to give her acceptance speech. She said, "I was a 16 year-old mother in a home for unwed mothers, but that's alright — it's just material for a testimony". She said, "I remember being abused by a family member, but that's alright too — it's just material for a testimony". She went on to make other statements and as she spoke, I sat there thinking about what she was saying — we all have material for a testimony.

Testimony — Webster's Dictionary states that a testimony is an outward sign, an open acknowledgement, evidence, witness, and firsthand authentication of a fact. Last and most meaningful of all definitions is "a public profession of a religious experience". 2 Timothy 1:8-10 states: "Therefore do not be ashamed of the testimony of our Lord, nor of me His prisoner, but share with me in the sufferings for the gospel according to the power of God, who has saved us and called *us* with a holy calling, not according to our works, but according to His own purpose and grace which was given to us in Christ Jesus before time began, but has now been revealed by the appearing of our Savior Jesus Christ, *who* has abolished death and brought life and immortality to light through the gospel..." This scripture starts out saying, "So do not be ashamed of the testimony of our Lord". It also states that having a testimony is not because of anything we have done, but because of God's own purpose and grace for us. Believe me, it can be difficult to share your testimony

— sometimes, we think more of the embarrassment we may feel by revealing intimate details, rather than thinking how those words may deter someone else from getting into the same situation that we were in. Thank God, we can call on the Holy Spirit to give us courage.

Comedians are always looking for material to make their audience laugh and come alive. They may find the story in their families, children, spouse, friends, co-workers or even their enemies. When a seamstress looks for material, she looks for color, pattern, width, yardage, texture and weight. We don't have to look for material for our testimonies for they are given to us as a part of our individual lives. Some material is good and some can be labeled as battle scars — things we had to go through to get to where we are today. Trials and tribulations — the good times and the bad, give us this material for a testimony. But, there is something that you should know: even though God isn't the author of these trials and tribulations, there are times when He may allow them to happen to give us this material for a testimony. After giving us this material, He gives us a way out for a testimony. I Corinthians 10:13 declares, "No temptation has overtaken you except such as is common to man; but God is faithful, who will not allow you to be tempted beyond what you are able, but with the temptation will also make the way of escape that you may be able to bear it." Our testimonies are important to the work of God. It's our way of being a witness to the goodness of the Lord. James 1:2 — "Consider it pure joy, my brothers, whenever you face trials of many kinds." Instead of complaining about our struggles, we should see them as opportunities for growth and witnessing. We have to ask God to help us to solve our problems and to give us the strength to endure them. Then be patient. God will not leave you alone with your problems: He will stay close and help us to grow through the test.

This book is my personal testimony. In telling my story, I have been able to heal from a lot of pain from my past. The struggles, pain and times of joy that I incurred have given me my material for this testimony. Today, I want to share everything that I have learned with you. My prayer is that it helps you to get through whatever situation you are struggling to get through this day and every day of your blessed life!

Theresa M. Odom-Surgick

CHAPTER 1

My Family Structure

"For I know him, that he will command his children and his household after him, and they shall keep the way of the LORD, to do justice and judgment; that the LORD may bring upon Abraham that which he hath spoken of him." Genesis 18:19

Being raised in a Christian home with two of the most loving parents — Benjamin Odom, born in Savannah, Georgia — raised in Allendale County, South Carolina and Delila Melrose Jacobs of Florence, South Carolina was a most memorable experience for me and my two sisters — Denise and Rose; and my brother, Benjamin. We were very happy!

Looking back at the way we were raised, mom and dad were really an example of what real parenthood is all about. They didn't just leave us to our own devices, but they were there to make sure that we worked to the best of our ability to be all that we could be in every way. I remember how mom sat with me at the kitchen table as I learned to write in cursive; making me write my name over and over again until it looked good, was straight and on the line. They were great parents, nuturing us and showing their love in every way to each one of us.

I can honestly say that I can never, ever remember hearing my mom and dad have angry words toward each other — at least not in front of us children.

There were days that dad would load us up in the car and take us to Carvel's for a soft served ice cream cone. Some Saturdays, we'd even go to the drive-in movie and eat hot dogs and popcorn. Once a year during the summer, he would take us to Story Town, now called the Great Escape — and let's not forget those family vacations to Philadelphia, PA to visit Aunt Gertrude and the family. I thank God for my Dad, because even though he didn't have a "normal" family upbringing, he made sure that we did. I am not sure about the circumstances, but at the age of 6 months old, my dad was taken from his parents, Ben Odom and Maggie Lewis and raised by his Aunt Gertrude. Being separated from his sisters and brothers took away the love and relationship he should have had from knowing his siblings. Today, he still has no idea where they are or even if they still exist.

At Christmas time, in addition to our toys, we would receive a brown paper bag, full of fruit, hard candy and nuts to snack on. Whether it was just sitting outside on the porch of our home at

242 Second Street, eating together at the dinner table or going to Washington Park on a warm Sunday afternoon, my parents really knew the value of real family time — something that is missing from many of today's modern families.

On Sundays we were up early in the morning getting ready for a full day at church — the Mount Olive Southern Missionary Baptist Church, where my then, future husband's father, Reverend Odell Wesley Surgick, was the Pastor.

Most people and pastors in Albany, NY and surrounding areas knew or heard about O.W. Surgick. He was friends with judges, attorneys and many city officials because of the love and care he showed for the downtrodden. He would make it his business to go to the court house every day and make sure that people were treated fairly within the court system. No matter where he went, people would shout out to him and if he had a dollar in his pocket, it was yours. When he passed away, there was talk of naming North Pearl Street in his honor — sad to say, it never happened.

Sunday was the busiest day in our household; we would first go to Sunday school, and then to morning service. Some Sundays, in addition to the regular morning service, we would go to BTU (Baptist Training Union) in the evening. My mom was the director of music at the church. She taught the choirs and played the piano for the Choresters, Senior Choir and the Youth Choir which was then called, of all things, "The Chubby Choir" — don't ask me where that name came from, but we were called the Chubby Choir. Years later, the name was changed to the Catherine Surgick Choir, after our Pastor's wife, my mother-in-law.

Reverend Odell Wesley and Catherine Surgick

We were always in church and the church was in our home. There were many times when mom had choir rehearsal at our house also inviting choir members and friends to the house for gatherings. When my mom retired from the music ministry, she turned the choir ministry over to me and my brother, Benjamin; he played the organ and I taught songs and directed the choir. When my brother was 18, he got an opportunity to play bass guitar for J.J. Farley and the Original Soul Stirrers at the Arbor Hill Community Center for a concert.

The day after the concert, we were told that he had left home and was on the road with the Soul Stirrers. Today, he is their manager, songwriter/music arranger, lead singer and bass player.

The music was in us at an early age, inherited — it was in our blood. Everyone in our family could either sing or play some kind of musical instrument — uncles, aunts, cousins, grandpa — they all had some gift of music. So it goes without saying that mom and dad would take us and form a family singing group with the four of us children — the Odom Singers — singing in perfect harmony.

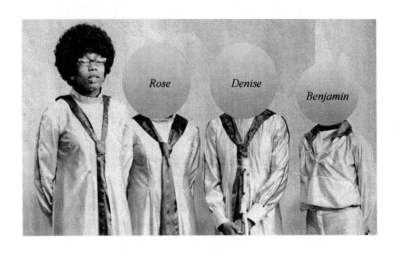

Rose Denise Benjamin

Mom taught us every harmony and dad recorded the songs on the old reel to reel and videotaped. We enjoyed singing and traveling all over to different churches, colleges and Christian events in and around the New York area and even out of state appearing on programs and performing concerts. We even sang regularly on television with a well known local personality, Mr. Artis Kitchen. He had a long running gospel program which aired on Sunday mornings. His closing quote for the program was, "be careful of the way you treat those on your way up, for they are the same ones you will meet on your way down".

Mom taught us everything from hymns to gospel music, even taking some secular songs and changing up the lyrics. She loved all kinds of music; one of her favorite gospel artists was Reverend James Cleveland. My favorite song that she taught us from his collection of songs was "In the Garden". On holidays, we would get together with our extended family — grandpa, cousins, aunts and uncles at my Aunt Bay's house laughing at Grandpa's not so funny jokes and eating my Aunt's homemade baking powder biscuits and Sweet Potato Pies. Some of us would hide her pies to take home later and those who didn't get the chance to sneak a pie would argue over who would get to take the last pie.

Aunt Bay and Shawne

Flipping through the pages of an old hymn book, we would harmonize — everyone jumping right in on soprano, alto, tenor, baritone or bass. Jacobs Descendants are who we were — descendants of Algue and Emma Melrose Jacobs.

Grandpa, Algue Jacobs and Krystal

From the youngest to the oldest, we would end our family time together singing a medley of songs with Grandpa as he led us in a round of spiritual songs and hymns. While sitting or standing around him, he would lead us singing songs like "Beulah Land" and "Standing in the Need of Prayer".

As with any family circle, we had our times of joy and tragedy. As a child, I still remember playing outside on North Pearl Street, while my great- great grandmother, Janie Mae Jacobs, watched over us from the top of her porch. To then hear her voice of anguish one warm summer night, shattering through the voices of children playing, people laughing and conversing is still so vivid in my mind as she was told that her youngest daughter, Flossie, who was my Grand

Aunt affectionately known as Aunt Sis was killed in a drunk driving, racing accident. My Uncle George and another person were racing on their way back from Saratoga Springs, NY. I thank God that my parents had opted out from traveling to Saratoga on that tragic day. My Uncles and even my Grandfather had a penchant for drinking. On several occasions we children would make it a game of hiding the alcohol from them when at Aunt Bay's house during family gatherings. How angry that would make the elders; we would end up giving it back to them and watch as they would drink themselves silly — that's when the jokes and laughter were most prominent.

Mom as a teenager with Flossie "Aunt Sis"

Another time, Grandpa was in a serious accident and we almost lost him. Somehow, he had lost his footing and fell down an embankment while fishing. As a result, he fell into a coma. The doctors tried to encourage my mom and Aunt Janie, my mom's sister, to remove him from the life support machine — they both said "No!"

Aunt Janie and Mom

Days later, Grandpa opened His eyes — miracle of miracles! That really taught me a lesson that I will never forget — God alone has control of our lives and we have to let Him have that control — He is the ultimate decision maker for everything concerning our lives. It's not up to us to dictate our fate; it is God who makes the final decision. Many years later, Grandpa went home to be with God. I believe I was the last family member to see him alive. I had gone to the nursing home and sat with him in his room. He didn't know I was there that evening. In the quietness of that room, I stood next to his bed and softly whispered hymns of praise in his ear. A little while after returning home from his bedside, I received a call saying that he had passed away. I was sad, but glad that I had gone there and had spent those last peaceful hours with him — alone, just the two of us and the angels of God standing guard making preparation to take his spirit away. It feels good to have been a part of that solemn, but joyful occasion.

Then there was my precious niece, Patrice who died at the age of 13. While my mom was visiting my sister, Denise in Maryland, she went into the bedroom to see her first baby granddaughter and found her lying there lethargic, eyes glazed. After coming home from the hospital, Patrice had been continuously crying and was refusing to eat. Her breathing was heavy and she laid there just staring blankly when my mom found her.

Patrice Gabourel, my Niece

After several tests, the doctors diagnosed her with Maple Syrup Urine Disease and said that it was the worst case they had seen. Things were touch and go for a while with trying to get her to eat. They found she had no gag reflex and would not take any food by mouth. Finally, a decision to insert a gastric tube was made and they began feeding directly into her stomach not expecting her to live long. The doctors tried to encourage my sister and her husband to put Patrice into a special needs facility because they said that she would never walk, talk or even recognize the family. God proved the doctors wrong and we saw her walking, holding conversations being very talkative and even dancing. With her beautiful voice, she even led songs in the youth choir at church. When she led the song "Now Behold the Lamb", there was such a beautiful presence in the atmosphere. I just loved hearing her call my name with her sweet, precious voice. She was a very loving child and was very near and dear to the heart of all who knew her — she touched a lot of lives in her short life. She lived longer than the doctors expected. Only God has the authority to make life's important decisions. He has proved Himself over and over again.

My Nieces, Patrice and Tiffany

A MESSAGE TO THE READER:

Family and the time we spend with each other are so important. I have heard of persons who have gotten into arguments with family members and have stopped speaking to each other for a number of years. Forgiveness is a necessity in any relationship, otherwise, anger and hard feelings are misplaced. Love has to be the guiding factor in any family. Not being able to forgive leaves a blemish in your life that keeps you tied to the hurt and pain that eventually turns to gangrene if you let it sit too long. We should love unconditionally, just as God loves us. You may not like the way a person acts or the things that are done, but you have to love them — it will outshine the darkness that you may find hard to cope with. Your family structure will help guide the way you live, relate to others and raise your family. Love and forgive as you are loved and forgiven by God.

CHAPTER 2

My Faith Tested

"Fear thou not; for I am with thee: be not dismayed; for I am thy God: I will strengthen thee; yea, I will help thee; yea, I will uphold thee with the right hand of my righteousness". Isaiah 41:10

1995 was a very unforgettable — uncomfortable year. It started out well for me as I took early retirement from Bell Atlantic. There was such great excitement in my heart when walking away from the building where I worked for a little over 23 years — a building where I had made so many memories; some good and some bad.

Getting my feet into the door to work in a small steno unit in the basement at 158 State Street in Albany, NY proved to be a true blessing — a place where my mom had already been working for many years; I was now following in her footsteps. In walking through those double glass doors my very first day of work, I reminisced about the times that mom would take us, as children, to the annual Christmas parties in the basement of that same tall, gray, brick building which sat across from the capitol in the heart of the city. Year after year, she would take us dressed up in our Sunday's best and go to this annual event.

Mom was just as excited as we were when taking us to see Santa Claus, eat cookies, candy, drink punch and smile as she showed us off to her many friends. One time we were even asked to sing a song. The biggest joy for me was when Santa gave out the gifts. I would pensively watch the other children opening their gifts waiting and watching to see if somehow, I could get handed the biggest box. It was so much fun! And now, as an adult, I would actually be working in that same basement office!

Checking in with the receptionist at the front desk on my first day of work, my heart overflowed with even more joy as I delighted in the fact that I would actually be working in the same building with my mom. I would be having lunch with her, going for walks, having our girl talks; oh yes, it was going to be exciting working with my mom.

Mom and I were the best of friends: a true team. We did everything together — travel, sing, compose songs, exercise and even took up belly dancing and African dance lessons. The two of us were a sight to behold as we danced across the floor at times almost falling out from exhaustion! We also took a poetry writing class to help with our song writing skills.

I have so many fond memories of the times that we shared together. I remember one day we went to Korvettes, a little shopping mall that used to be on Central Avenue in Colonie, NY where Targets now stands. Pregnant with my first child, Arnold DeShawne, the two of us went shopping at a sale for pillows and blankets.

Laughing, talking, joking, eating — we were having such a good time together. After getting our pillows and blankets, we walked out into the front parking lot, and as I unlocked the car door, a thought suddenly occurred to me; "Mom, we didn't pay for anything." What a sight it was to see the two of us running as fast as our feet could carry us — me with my big, round belly — trying to get back into the store before officials noticed and sent the security team after us. We were laughing all the way. The cashier at the register didn't find it as funny as we did when we told her what had just occurred — she didn't even crack a smile — she just went on about her business, looking at us with much suspicion. I cannot even begin to imagine what would have happened if we had gotten caught in that mess! Who would believe us? Angels were truly with us that day. What would I look like, pregnant in jail with my precious mom — the two of us caught behind bars? It's too scary to even think about!

Mom soon retired and I was left alone on the job; loneliness set in.

Taking lunch alone and walks alone, I was soon able to adapt and get into the routine of things, finding people to converse with and take walks. Then, the unthinkable happened — mom was diagnosed with breast cancer. I was devastated. Mom had never confided in me about finding the lump. I guess it was her way of shielding and protecting me from the hurt and pain she knew I would feel in hearing this devastating news — she knew how it would affect me.

As we were walking at lunch time, Latharee, one of mom's friends, informed me about what mom had revealed to her. When I was given this news, it was as if I heard her, but didn't really hear — shock blocked my comprehension. After this revelation had set in and with much contemplation, I concluded when mom had found the lump. You see, our family journeyed together to Orlando, Florida for a two-week family vacation. One particular day during this time, everyone planned to go to an amusement park and mom decided that she just wanted to stay at the villa — she said she didn't feel well. When we returned, I asked her what was wrong but she wouldn't tell me. I could tell by the expression on her face that something was seriously wrong; but she wouldn't tell me — her look failed to conceal her worry. I guess that's an attribute I get from her when it comes to my own facial expressions — when I'm worried, you see it; when I'm feeling depressed — you see it; when something is wrong — you see it written all over my face. I know without a shadow of a doubt — that was the day mom discovered the lump in her breast! That was a day that would forever change our lives.

An appointment was made for a biopsy and we accompanied mom to get the results. Sitting and waiting in the small exam room were the four of us — my sister Rose and I were sitting side by side; dad was on the other side of the room and mom was seated on the exam table. The doctor came in and greeted us and after his preliminary introduction and a short pause, those fateful, ugly words came spewing from his mouth — "It's malignant." Mom gasped and put her hands to her face; dad sat there for a second, then got up and went to a little, white pedestal sink over in the corner of the room and threw water on his face. I sat there stunned, unable to move or react. Rose sat there, just as paralyzed as I. It seemed as if our perfect world had just stopped revolving, collapsed and crushed in on us; the happy Christian family we knew had just been tossed like a Frisbee into a whirlwind of hurt, confusion and disbelief. I could not believe it! My mom, a precious, God fearing, loving and kind woman, who I loved and adored dearly, had "malignant" cancer. How could this happen? Where was God in all of this? As the doctor proceeded to examine mom, Rose and I stood up and walked out. I was the oldest sibling in the family, but I could hardly contain myself as we stepped outside of the examination room. Rose, my youngest sister, began to encourage and admonish me — "We've got to hold it together for mom! We can't let her see us upset! She's got to get through this!"

About a month later, mom had a radical mastectomy — followed by months of chemotherapy. I got permission from my supervisor and changed my work schedule so that I could go with her every Tuesday morning for her chemotherapy treatments. I needed to be there to make sure she was okay and then take her home because of those dreadful side effects. Chemo took its toll on mom — losing her hair, nausea, weight loss; they had to put a catheter in her chest to feed the Tamoxifen into her frail body. My poor mom — all I could do was pray and ask God for His healing virtue to flow through her just like the woman in the Bible, who had the issue of blood. I remember purchasing a set of cassette tapes by John Hagee that had scriptures on healing read aloud and told mom to listen to them continually. Some months later, the cancer was in remission!! Mom was back to her old self — singing, traveling and even teaching lessons at the church at which she was one of the founders — The Star of Bethlehem.

About six years or more passed by and all went well.....But not for long. Mom was in the kitchen cooking and ever so nonchalant she said, "The cancer has returned". I sat there stunned by her words as she continued to say, "Everybody has to die, I'm just going to die sooner". That day, a day that had been a good day for me, ended up being one of the worse days of my life. I had planned to go home and cook a big meal for my family, but ended up leaving and shutting myself up in my room crying.....Praying...Questioning God...And crying even more.

Through it all, I recalled this scripture about seasons. *Ecclesiastes 3:1-11 To everything there is a season, and a time to every purpose under the heaven: A time to be born, and a time to die; a time to plant, and a time to pluck up that which is planted; A time to kill, and a time to heal; a time to break down, and a time to build up; A time to weep, and a time to laugh; a time to mourn, and a time to dance; A time to cast away stones, and a time to gather stones together; a time to embrace, and a time to refrain from embracing; A time to get, and a time to lose; a time to keep, and a time to cast away; A time to rend, and a time to sew; a time to keep silence, and a time to speak; A time to love, and a time to hate; a time of war, and a time of peace. What profit hath he that worketh in that wherein he laboureth? I have seen the travail, which God hath given to the sons of men to be exercised in it. He hath made everything beautiful in his time: also he hath set the world in their heart, so that no man can find out the work that God maketh from the beginning to the end.* More Chemotherapy treatments were started.

Winter, February 15, 1995, was a rehearsal night for the Odell Wesley Surgick Ensemble; a singing group that I started with singers from different churches in the capital district and surrounding areas.

We were pretty good for a bunch of non-professional singers and mom was the senior member of the group. It was rare for her to miss a rehearsal. She was always there — standing right in front with the rest of the Sopranos — very expressive, singing her heart out. But on this particular night, she didn't show up and didn't call. Where is mom? Why didn't she come to rehearsal tonight? This really was not like her at all! After rehearsal I stopped at her home and she was sitting in the family room. Months before, I sat in that same room and announced to mom that God had spoken to me and was calling me to ministry. Mom was so excited — She said to me, "I knew it… I just knew it." The expression on her face was priceless as she took in what I had just said. Mom and dad were always a great support for us children. Whatever we did, wherever we went, they were there. It was that love and mentoring that is very instrumental in my ministry today. This news was a great joy to my mom and was my official acceptance of the call on my life. We were now in that same room with mom sitting in her favorite chair with a hot pack on the side of her head and neck. At that time, I didn't know it, but she was in serious pain. She tried to temper the situation by saying that it was just a neck pain. So we talked for a while and then I left.

About 1 a.m. that the morning, my sister Rose called and said that the ambulance was on its way to take mom to the hospital. During the night, she had awakened and was talking a lot of gibberish and trying to pull her clothes off. Rose picked me up from home and we rushed to the hospital and got there just in time to meet the ambulance. I could not believe what I was seeing. I was just talking to her. What was happening to my mom? No God! Please — I began to pray. I refused to believe that this was happening. Dear God, what is this?

As the light of a new day dawned with sunlight peeking through the hospital room blinds, the doctor slowly came in and upon greeting us, he said, "The cancer has spread to her brain. Later on today, we would like to begin radiation treatments." No! This cannot be true! I cannot accept this! Why God? Why? What happened to cause this? I had to stay focused and strong because I felt that if I didn't, it would show a lack of faith and belief in God and in what He could do — if He did it before, He would do it again! I was determined to believe and I had to stay strong. In my mind, I had to believe that mom was not going to die — this was not her season to die — the treatments just had to work again!

After a few treatments, the doctors sat our family down at the conference room table and said that the cancer was now also in her kidneys and liver — they began to talk about hospice care. I didn't want to talk to them nor did I want to hear what they had to say — I didn't want to discuss the subject of imminent death in any way, shape or form because in discussing it, they were giving up hope and I didn't want anyone to give up on my mother! God had to heal her! In my mind, as long as she was still here on this earth, there was still hope for a miracle; I just didn't want to believe that she was beyond a cure — God had to heal my mom! I refused to give up!

Even as I stayed at mom's side in that hospital room at Albany Medical Center, I studied God's word preparing for a message that I was asked to teach on the aspects and essence of praise and worship. As I got more into God's Word, He began to minister to me in music. As I hummed the music which He was giving to me, the lyrics soon followed from the scriptures. I was learning words like "Tehillah" — to sing, to laud. It's a spontaneous new song as you sing from a melody in your heart by adding words to it. It refers to a special kind of singing — it is singing prophetically straight to God an unpre-pared, unrehearsed song. It brings tremendous unity to the body of Christ. I also learned "Halal" — to shine; to make a show, to boast; to be clamorously foolish; and to celebrate. I sang this song to my mother as God gave it to me. It gave me a peacefulness that is hard to explain — it was the peace of God.

We took mom home and she was administered in-home hospice care.

Along with the hospice nurse, Aunt Janie, my mom's sister took such great care of her making sure that she was clean and had everything that she needed. On the day I was to minister on praise and worship, mom went home to be with the Lord — March 21, 1995. In studying and writing that song, which is entitled, "Your Majesty", I learned that — no matter the situation — even in the adversity and the death of a loved one, you will survive; God will give you His peace that is beyond any comprehension. As you minister to Him, He will minister to you. As you bless Him, He will in turn, bless you; God will inhabit your praise and worship. As I studied His word and sang that song in my mom's hospital room and in her home where we set up a hospital bed in the room where my ministry call was announced, God gave her a peace and calmness in her body. In this, He also gave me that peace — a perfect peace that really does surpass all understanding.

On the day she died, the hospice nurse came in and said, "It won't be long...It will be sometime today...Her limbs are very cold. Even though you don't know whether she can hear you or not, you should talk to her and let her know that everything is okay". So I did — "Mom its okay...We're going to be just fine...Don't worry about us" I said, choking back the tears. It got very late in the evening, so I left. Early in the morning before daybreak, Rose called — mom was gone.

Those days before mom died, she would just lay there — no words or movement; I never knew if she was hearing my songs of praises to God, but inspite of it all I sang knowing that the word of God is true — He dwells in your praise. We needed His peace that surpasses all understanding. Now I'm not saying that I was continually peaceful during the time of her suffering. There was one particular time before mom died that members of the church and the Pastor had to pick me up from the floor because I had completely lost it. I was so completely overwhelmed with what was happening to my mom; having to watch her die day by day in that hospital room had consumed me. My Pastor, at that time, was god sent at a most vulnerable time in my life. When mom passed away, I remember how she took me and my hurt and even though we were the same age, she mothered me; helping me to get past the hurt and loneliness of it all. I remember the day she took me shopping to buy a dress for me to wear to mom's funeral. We spent the entire day together. She helped to keep my mind off of the events that would most certainly take place within the next few days — preparing the funeral service, picking the casket and burial place, calling relatives and friends. This pastor is a very compassionate person and she tried her best to make sure that I was okay.

I was consumed with grief and despair. There was a few mothers' day where I could barely function. Pastor had to remind me that I too was a mother and that I needed to be celebrated. I needed to let my children — Krystal, Andrae, Antoine and Shawne celebrate me!

But, I was a total wreck! I had gone into a deep depression — my mom — my buddy was gone and I felt so alone.

Nothing anyone could say helped me at this point. Mom was gone. She was no longer here! I remembered a time when I had suffered a miscarriage and was deeply depressed and my mom was the one who was there to help get me out of that depression by saying to me, "make a list of all of the good things that God has brought your way and compare it to the negative. I know that the good will outweigh the bad." Now, I was alone and I had to put all of my trust in God — He alone would have to bring me out of this — I had a choice to make — live or mentally, physically and spiritually die.

MY TWO-FOLD MESSAGE TO THE READER:

#1) Mom and I had a strong relationship. A child, having real relationships with parents is so important to the health, growth and well-being of that child. But, there is a line that must be drawn so that the child does not forget that you are the parent and that there is a greater level of respect that has been earned and is deserved. I've seen so many examples of children who have gone to the level of treating that parent like one of their friends and at times, becoming very disrespectful. Parenthood has to come first and then comes friendship. The word is true; when you raise a child in the way he should go, he will not depart from it. He may stray a little at times, but because you have raised him under right standards, he will at some point return to what he has been taught under your parenting and God's word.

#2) Life brings with it some good times and bad. It's all a part of our journey to our ultimate destiny as human beings on this earth. It's all about how we handle our individual situations. We can either let them control us, or we can control them with God's help. His infinite wisdom will help us get through our hard times of trials and pain. It's never easy so don't let anyone ever lay a guilt trip on you when in the grieving process. That time is always needed in order to let go of the pain and hurt of your loss. The question for you to answer is, "how long will you grieve?" That's up to you. Make a choice to live or mentally, physically and spiritually die.

CHAPTER 3

My Will To Live Tested

"The right hand of the LORD is exalted: the right hand of the LORD doeth valiantly. I shall not die, but live, and declare the works of the LORD. The LORD hath chastened me sore: but he hath not given me over unto death." Psalm 118:16-18

I was living a life that in my own eyes was not fulfilling. I was always questioning what my purpose was and being made to feel like a complete failure at things I was assigned to. One Sunday after church I came home feeling very tired and stressed because my mind had been filled with so much troubling mess; I was overwhelmed to no end. One of the things that took me to the edge was a leadership meeting that I had to attend. It was at that meeting that I found out that after years of being the minister of music, my service was no longer needed in that capacity. It would have been different if I had received a memo, a note or even a phone call to let me know ahead of time so that my mind could have been prepared for this announcement… but it didn't happen that way. I found out the day of the meeting along with a room full of upper leadership as the announcement was made congratulating the new minister. This was a devastating, embarrassing moment for me. Once again, I was made to feel like I had failed at another task that had been placed into my hands. Music was in my blood — how could I now not be meeting all of the requirements that it took for this ministry? This was just one of the things that took me to the point of not wanting to live anymore — I was a failure.

That Sunday when I came home from church, I went straight to my living room couch and lay down and prayed, "Lord, just let me sleep so that I don't have to think". Have you ever been there before? It had gotten to the point where I had been thinking strongly about death — how death would be the easy way out. I needed some peace, and death at that moment, was the only option that I thought would bring me some much needed peace. So I prayed for sleep, which God gave to me.

As I fell into a deep sleep, I dreamed. God took me to a church — a large brick, gray stone building sitting on a hill surrounded by lush green grass. Inside the church, we were having choir rehearsal. The musician, a lady named Mary, was playing the introduction to a song. When she completed the introduction, we all began singing "King of my life I crown Thee now... Thine shall the glory be...Lest I forget Thine thorn crowned brow, lead me to Calvary." When we finished singing that stanza, Mary stopped playing and said, "I wasn't playing that song; I was playing something else." I then ran out of the church, with my hymn book in hand trying to find out what she was playing. Now don't ask me why I ran out of the church, but when I returned, the place was empty — everyone had left. Where did the choir go — where did Mary, the musician go?

I woke up from my dream with no viable answer to my question. For days, that song rang in my head. I constantly asked God, "What is the meaning of this dream?" Why did everyone leave? In my questioning, on a daily basis, God would give me bits and pieces of the meaning of this weird dream. He showed me how the enemy had played a trick on me and how he was purposefully distracting me sending me on a tangent. Satan was messing with my mind — taking my focus off of my purpose.

God showed me how everyone in that rehearsal, including myself knew the song that the musician was playing, but because of deception, the enemy was able to bring in confusion. There had been so much confusion in my life during the previous months — still feeling the impact of the death of my mom, family and finance issues, church issues and self issues were going crazy in my head and making me want to sleep and think about death as an end to my peace less life. I had even thought about getting an airplane ticket to wherever I could go and not tell anyone — not even my family. I would start a brand-new life and find a church, just sit in the congregation and not do anything. That's the kind of confusion and craziness that was in my mind.

Many times, the cares of life can push you to the limit and if you are weak from the turmoil and stress, it is no trouble at all getting you to the place of forgetting to put your total trust and faith in God. You get weak and tired in your mind and it becomes the battleground for Satan. He pulls and stretches you until you give in and can't be stretched anymore. I was in the church encouraging others while putting on my mask of deception when in their presence and when by myself, I felt like I would lose my mind. When going through this, the one thing that could not be taken from me was my praise — so I went to church and I sang knowing that God dwells in the praise of His people.

You may recall that the song heard in my dream was "Lead Me to Calvary" — well, God was showing me that I was going through my own personal Calvary. Calvary was a place of indecision, pain, struggle, embarrassment, anguish and agony. I was in my own personal Calvary — about to lose my house, not knowing where we would live; living from paycheck to paycheck; engine on my car had just died; marriage about to break up, but no one knew because I continued to put on the good face and come in as if nothing were wrong — My presence was there, but in mind, I was not present. That was my Calvary.

Walking through my Calvary, I had lost focus. That dream was a wake up call from God. In the chorus of that song, the lyrics say, "Lest I forget Gethsemane, lest I forget Thine agony, lest I forget Thy love for me, lead me to Calvary." I had taken my eyes off of God and had lost all faith so I was deceived — tricked by the enemy and led into my own Calvary. I knew the name of the song — I was a praiser and just because man tried to shut me down and the difficulties of life had torn me up, there was still no need for me to give up... there is always a better way out — it was up to me to find a positive way. I had to live and not die — I had to make the choice to recognize who God was and what He could do in and with my life; I was not a failure and this depression had to go!

MY MESSAGE TO THE READER

Although my story of depression does not yet end here, I wanted to give you some steps to victory that I finally learned which helped me to cope with this tested life. They are outlined in 2nd Chronicles 20 (please read it). When the enemy comes in and tries to threaten and destroy you, this is what you have to do:

1. Fear the Lord (reverence Him).
2. Fast
3. Pray: Meditate on who God is. Have an awareness of the Christ who dwells in you
4. Position yourself to hear (set the atmosphere with a song of praise)
5. Listen for the voice of God
6. Stand still (don't get so interrupted or tested that you can't hear)
7. Worship and praise God no matter what the circumstance
8. Believe God's Word and
9. Praise, Praise, Praise and bless the Lord for your victory — you shall live and not die![1]

---

1   *"Lead Me To Calvary"* — *Written by Jennie E. Hussey (1921) Music by William J. Kilpatrick*

CHAPTER 4

My Patience With God Tested

"Wait on the Lord: be of good courage, and he shall strengthen thine heart: wait, I say, on the Lord". Psalm 27:14

Desperation and depression led to a separation in my marriage of 32 years. At the time we had been married, I had taken so much — it seemed like we were always struggling.

My husband had the tendency to raise his voice at me in conversation and how I despised him for that — it would irritate me so much. We also always struggled financially to the point where, after purchasing our first home we had to file bankruptcy and lost that home to foreclosure. I couldn't take it anymore, so when we were forced to move out of that home, I politely told him, "Krystal and I are moving to Latham". That was my cold way of letting him know that he was no longer in the picture — he would not be moving in with us.

Looking around, I was seeing how others were moving ahead and being prosperous — they seemed so successful and happy. We were going nowhere — our credit was horrendous; no joy — no peace — not one thing to show for all of our years of marriage! Where was my faith? I was miserable. It had gotten to the point that I did not want to be anywhere near him — I didn't want him touching me; every time he did, I felt like I was being raped and violated — I just wanted to be free and on my own. I wanted to get my life back on track and felt like that would not happen with him around. Proving my point, I moved into a house and paid — on my own — $1,400 a month for rent, in addition to paying other important bills. Krystal and I were happy and had some semblance of peace. At this point, I felt so independent and so free. I was a survivor; a single mom able to raise my daughter without the stress and struggle that I had felt for so long — I was even able to lose weight and got down to a size 14. Although it was late in the game, I was also able to open a college fund through the NYS College Fund program for my baby girl.

Over time, things changed and I had to remember that God is the one who holds your destiny in the palm of His hands. Sometimes it takes getting away from a situation to help you grow and mature. Being by myself really taught me how to lean on God. It was really self empowering to know that I could really survive as I leaned and trusted in God. In life, I had never taken advantage of the opportunity that comes once you have graduated from high school and leave your parents' nest; there was no testing out how it felt to be a responsible young adult. I had gone from my parent's house, right into marriage — never traveling alone, going away to college or having my own apartment — this was a great experience for me. In doing so, I learned a lot about myself. I learned who I was and the things I had to change within myself in order to be a good wife, mother and steward. It wasn't entirely his fault...I had some responsibility in the failure of our marriage; this separation gave me time to think, live and learn a few things. Knowing this, I learned to get along, alone and I survived.

Separation lasted for almost two years. I began to feel lonely and needed a man's touch. Can you believe that I actually registered on E Harmony? I looked at the website a couple of times but it just wasn't for me — I was still married...I wanted him back; I missed him....With all of the challenges we had suffered, we still had a lot invested in each other. So I went running back to him. With counseling, talking and working out our different issues, we renewed our wedding vows in a beautiful ceremony. I even wrote a song that I sang to him at that ceremony that left people in awe and in tears as they listened to the lyrics. We were back together again and in love.

One in the Spirit & One in Love

When I first met you - we were children in church. My mom she played the keyboard - your dad he gave the word. Never knowing one day that their kids would be one - one in the spirit and one in love.

Even though the times have been rough

A separation incurred - Jesus He was there keeping love in us stirred. Having done all we could do- The Lord would see us through so we could be one in the spirit, one in love.

Life has not been fair - many trials, pains and cares. But Jesus took His time, keeping us in line. So that when we returned together again, we'd be one in the spirit - yes, one in love.

We're in love again - It's like the first time we met. A love so deep inside forever to abide. A love that only we can embrace that no one can erase.

We are one in the spirit, yes - one in love.

As I said, God is the one who holds your destiny in the palm of His hands and I truly believe that it was God who had a hand in getting us back together again; if we had not, my husband probably would not be alive today. Because of my encouragement and making him go for a physical, we found out that he was sick with Prostate Cancer. It was very devastating causing a test of my faith; where would all of this head and how would it end. I had to stay strong for my husband and here I was again trying to stay strong — first my mom and now for my husband. He wasn't saying much, but I knew that he was thinking a lot. My husband can be a jokester at times; quite the clown — but he became very quiet. There was no music in our lives at this time; there was no song to sing in our sadness. Once again, Cancer had reared its ugly head up in our family. My husband's family also has had a history of Cancer with his mom. I tried not to think too hard about what could happen — trying not to think about the past and the pain we went through with my mom. I didn't want to relive all that I had gone through and the hurt that we as a family had endured with her loss. How would this new story end?

James 1: 2-4 ~ "My brethren, count it all joy when you fall into divers temptations; Knowing this, that the trying of your faith worketh patience. But let patience have her perfect work, that you may be perfect and entire, wanting nothing". This adversity with my husband really put me to the test– patience had truly been produced in my life. Surgery was scheduled and according to the doctor, he would have it on Monday and be out of the hospital on Wednesday. The scenario didn't go according to plan. That Monday, we had to be in the hospital at 8 a.m. as preparation for the surgery which would begin at 12 noon. I sat with my children in the family reception area along with other persons who were waiting for their friends and loved ones to come out of surgery — waiting for the outcome. Waiting patiently — praying, reading scripture, talking to God; hoping, trusting and believing — thinking and battling in my mind with Satan. In times like these, the enemy likes to play mind games. With his help, I began thinking, "Will Arnold survive this? Will he be okay?" My faith was being tested once again. Time was slowly passing by; 12 noon turned to 2 o'clock — 2 to 4 o'clock — 4 o'clock turned to 6 o'clock and then finally the personal pager that was given to me vibrated in my hand and lit up.

As I approached the desk, the receptionist said to me, "The surgery nurse is on the phone and would like to speak with you". Listening attentively, the nurse then told me "the doctor is finishing up — everything went very well; we'll let you know when he is in recovery". I could not let loose of the pure joy that I was feeling fully until I could see my husband with my own eyes. So again, I sat down watching the clock — waiting patiently. The reception desk closed and finally Dr. Murray and his assistant headed my way. He repeated what the nurse had said, "Things went well", but then also stated — "it's a good thing we got it out. In the center of it was a more aggressive form of Cancer — all of his margins are good and we got it all out". As I walked back to my seat, praise welled up in my heart — one that was very hard to contain as the doctor walked away.

Still waiting, at around 9:30 p.m., they finally gave us the signal that it was okay to go up to the family recovery room. Once there, again we sat and waited. We were told that they were trying to get his pain under control. Every time we heard an elevator door open, Krystal, the youngest of our four children would run to see if it was her daddy they were bringing out. After a few false hopes, it was finally him — the father of my children and my husband of almost 34 years being rolled in on a stretcher — dressed mummified, wrapped in white blankets from head to toe. I wasn't prepared for what I saw. I didn't expect the man that I loved to be lying there in this horrifying state. So sedated that he couldn't even hear me calling his name, he didn't even know that the children and I were standing there excited to see him. The attendant who was escorting him saw through our feelings of shock and hurt as he said, "I'll let you know when you can come down to the room".

Again, we waited patiently as the nurse got him settled in his room. Finally, we got word. My youngest two children, Krystal, Antoine and I made our way to his room. My oldest son, Shawne, stayed back in the family room; he could not bear seeing his father in that condition. As we walked into the room — I looked at my husband and saw pain written all over his face. He was now awake with eyes wide open but it seemed as if he couldn't see me. I remember not being able to see the white of his eyes — he was talking, but babbling. You could hear the writhing of pain in his voice. One sentence that I could finally comprehend him saying was, "when I get better, I'm going to punch him for hurting me." It was funny, but I had no will to laugh — I was hurting to see him in so much pain. I hurried the children from the room not wanting them to see him in such a confused state of mind, due to the heavy doses of medication. I assured him that I would be there the next morning; Krystal and I cried all the way home.

I was there at the hospital at 6 a.m. that morning. I wanted to make sure I could see the doctor when he made his scheduled rounds. I made my way into his room and quietly sat watching my husband as he slept — again, waiting patiently. Isaiah 40:31 says, "But they that wait upon the LORD shall renew their strength; they shall mount up with wings as eagles; they shall run, and not be weary; and they shall walk, and not faint". The Hebrew word for "wait" is "qawah" which means to wait with the notion of holding on strong; and during the time becoming wound together with the object of the waiting. So, I waited — hoping and praying that this morning would bring about a change from all we had incurred the day before.

My husband awakened from his sleep — still in pain, but not as severe — not even remembering my presence the night before. I was glad that on this morning, he was in his right mind — he could see me and said "you look pretty"; I was dressed up, in a red suit, ready to go to work. I had pre-determined that I would wait until he came home from the hospital to take days off from work — I wanted to be there for him when the time was right.

Because of his pain, Morphine became his saving grace; it made him drowsy and made him sleep. So I went to work; that night I would not be getting out of work until 9 p.m. therefore, I was not able to return to the hospital. The next day, I went into my husband's room and he was not there — he had been moved. Where was he? Panic began to set in as I searched for an answer. No one had called to inform me of this sudden move. Why had he been moved? Finally getting an answer, I was told that he had been moved and taken to the ICU; his heart rate had gone completely off the chart. During the night as the nurse was checking his vital signs, his heart rate was racing so fast, she could not catch the rhythm of the heartbeat. Thinking something was wrong with the monitor, she got another nurse to check it. Sure enough, his heart rate was too fast to even check, so they moved him to ICU fearing the worse. Again, I patiently waited– waiting for something good to happen, so while I waited, I prayed for a miracle. I didn't want to lose him; I couldn't go through another loss. Would I be able to handle it?

Depending on the situation you are facing, waiting can cause many emotions to uproot in your spirit. In my case, there was fear, anticipation, anxiety, confusion, loneliness, stress, discouragement, hopelessness — all rolled up into one tight giant ball of emotional confusion. As I sat there — waiting — wanting the diagnosis to change, I was praying — believing and expecting a good report. The next day the doctor gave us more discouraging news — "there is a possibility that he will have to go on dialysis". Dialysis? He was going into renal failure — his kidneys weren't working properly. My God! What is happening? It's Wednesday; he was supposed to be coming home with me — why Lord...Why? The nurse said, "We're pumping gallons of fluid into him and nothing is coming out". Panic attack! She continues to say, "We're waiting to see if his kidney function will start to kick in. Many times it's all of the medication that is used during surgery that can cause this — but it is unusual for this to happen". Again — I wait — patiently waiting.

Dialysis? For how long? The doctor says, "Well we're hoping that one will do it and that it will force the kidneys to start functioning". I prayed and I prayed — trying to keep a positive outlook for my husband's sake. Most of the time I would just sit there watching as he lay there sedated with the Morphine. I had to make all major decisions and had to stay positive and prayed up. I could not fall apart but one of those days I actually did fall apart. I really needed someone to talk to, so I called one of the Ministers at church and she came and had lunch with me and we talked. She really took the time to encourage me, letting me know that it would be okay. I had to hold on, but how long Lord — how long? I need help — I'm getting tired of sitting here and watching a bag attached to the side of the bed to see if there's fluid in it and how much fluid. This bag was attached to a man who was once strong — a man who worked for years as a longshoreman at the Port of Albany; now it has come to this — and again, I wait.

Psalm 37: 7a says to "Rest in the LORD, and wait patiently for him". So I rested in the Lord — knowing without a shadow of a doubt that He does all things well and in His time. For He is a sovereign God. The day was far spent, so I went home. As I drove home, another war rose up in my mind. My mind was in a battle with Satan for my husband's life. He began to attack my thoughts with "what ifs". What if his kidneys don't kick in? What if he has to continue with dialysis? What if his body can't handle all of this? After all, he is a diabetic; will I lose him? God just brought us back together! I went home and in a panic, I called my Pastor — she listened, she encouraged me and she prayed. She knew the right words to say. She was the one who knew all I was going through, for she had been in my place. She knew the pain and heartache of seeing the man you love going through this type of major surgery — she knew the place I was in. Even though the setbacks of renal failure, blood sugar highs and lows and an irregular heart beat were all in place and much different from what she had experienced — she knew — God had prepared her to minister to me and a peace set in as I received that loving ministry.

The next morning, I was at the hospital even earlier. So many things were happening. Drugged with Morphine — he slept. He wasn't eating and had no appetite; therefore, his sugar levels were running rampant. He wasn't producing enough fluids to clear his kidneys; he was on heart medicine and a monitor — and now here I sat watching as they rolled in this giant machine to prepare him for dialysis. I began to question myself...Why wasn't God answering my prayers? This had been a big issue for me for so long — wondering if God heard my prayers. I remember how I prayed when my mom was sick with Cancer. I prayed so hard for her healing — but there was no earthly healing for her — so mom died. I remember feeling very helpless as I watched her go through the effects of Cancer and the Chemotherapy treatments each Tuesday. I remember how joyful we were when she went into remission — and sad when the Cancer returned. Why hadn't my prayers worked? Years later, I remember how the doctors took my sister and me into the family conference room and told us that there was nothing else they could do for her daughter, Patrice at age 13 — she was going to die. My sister and I left that conference room — went to and sat in her car and we began to pray powerfully, but Patrice still died.

It was after that — I began to question my effectiveness in prayer. What was I doing wrong? Why don't my prayers have any power? For a while, I would shun any activity at church that called for me to be an intercessor — in my eyes, my prayers were not packed with power. Finally, I had to come back to the realization that God is sovereign and He acts in His sovereign will. God can do what He wants — when He wants to and how we wants to at any given time. I had to come to terms with the fact that God has a sovereign will that must be accepted if we are to believe and have total faith and trust in Him. I had to remember that God always answers our prayers — not always in the way that we desire for them to be answered — but He answers them in His way and in His own time. It's up to us to accept His sovereign will in every situation — we have to accept God's perfect will.

While you wait and pray, you MUST have patience. The two go hand in hand. Yes, sometimes God will answer your prayer immediately and there are examples of that in the Bible, but there are also times when you have to wait — wait patiently for that answer — wait patiently for the outcome that is in the sovereign, divine, perfect will of God. Sometimes it may seem that He will hesitate to try your faith. He will put our faith under fire to see just where you stand in Him. My faith was under fire. It had not been long since my husband and I had reunited and now my husband was near death, not healing properly because he was a diabetic who had just come out of major cancer surgery. Recalling the scripture in James 1:4 that says, *"But let patience have her perfect work, that ye may be perfect and entire, wanting nothing"*. God is showing me how patience is playing out in my life even today. For so long there have been things that I have desired in my life that have not yet been fulfilled — so many desires. I tried to do things on my own, not letting God be the one to make sure those things happen for me in His own time. It was me trying to push things along. But God was trying to tell me — *"Not Now, not now but in My time things will begin to happen for you. Do you remember Abraham and Sarah? I didn't let them down. I am a God who honors His word — it never returns void — my word is true. Continue in my word and be obedient to My word and I will give you the desires of your heart. All will come to fruition. Continue in My faith and it will produce all that you need in life. Patiently wait and in due time, it shall come to pass."*

Prayer does work. It took many days of patience and faith, believing that God is a healer. God's work prevailed in my husband. Today, I look at him and know that my husband truly has the favor of God. Since the writing of this chapter, in March 2011 he had also had Double Pneumonia and then four months later had a heart/lung surgery which was also a scary situation in which they had to place him into a medically induced a coma. He is cancer free and his kidneys are functioning with no dialysis. We thought we were going to lose him a few times, but God has kept him safe in His arms. God is so good! We've gone through a lot; having gone through this battle with infirmity, we have grown even closer in love and faith in God. He does have heart arrhythmia and we are still praying that his heart will be totally healed. Testing is taking place to see what can be done to regulate his heart properly.

MY MESSAGE TO THE READER

Adversity takes on many forms. It's all a part of this life that each of us must live from day to day. Along with the abundant life that God desires for us comes our moments of challenges, stress, trials, tribulations, sadness and grief. Once the reality of any major situation or setback occurs, you have to make the choice to arrest any controlling emotions that may be a hindrance to you. Once you get the tears, and anger out — for however long, there must come a time that you have to stand up, straighten up your bowed down head and meet that situation head on and say, "No more! I will not let the emotion of it all take me out! I am not going to let this take full control of my life". Yes, there is a season for everything, but when God created man, he gave him the power of choice and YOU have to choose how long you want to wallow in the dirt and mud of that emotion and how long you want that season to last. You can choose to live or choose to die mentally, physically, emotionally and spiritually — it's up to you as to how long it will take to settle into the fact that — this crazy part of your life is over, has passed and is done with and then you decide how you want to handle those inevitable emotions. You can either stay there or walk away from it — pray and God will send you the comfort that you need to get over it. It's ultimately our choice! I do know that it's not an easy choice and I'm not making light of those emotions. Remember, I've been there and had my patience tested. As a result of all I've been through, I can honestly say that it is best to let go and let God have His way in your every situation. God will help you to handle it; just trust Him...You can do it!!

CHAPTER 5

My Spiritual Purpose

"For I know the thoughts that I think toward you,
saith the LORD, thoughts of peace, and not of evil,
to give you an expected end". Jeremiah 29:11

After being called into the ministry, I wanted and needed to grow.
There were times that I would shut myself up in my bedroom
and read and study God's word as I watched the TBN television
network, a Christian station. There would be such an awesome presence of God in my room that would cause me to cry out and dance
for joy. During that time, I was also introduced to a new group — a
Christian women's ministry. From that ministry grew a full gospel,
non-denominational church. It was something very new to me —
it was so different. The atmosphere was completely different from
what I had grown up with all of my life and was accustomed to.
Instead of the regular Baptist hymns and traditional songs they sang
more contemporary Christian music. Instead of the regular devo-
tional services, they had what was called praise and worship; it was
very charismatic. People were speaking in tongues and being slain in
the spirit. "What is this new religion?" I thought as I stood during a
praise and worship session. And this woman that stood before me
was so powerful in presenting the word — she was very convincing as she ministered. I stood watching as she very compassionately
hugged and was laying hands and praying for those that came up

for prayer. As I stood and watched what was happening before me, thoughts and emotions began stirring within me. I had never heard the word preached like this before and never heard these types of songs. Being overtaken with emotion, I began to cry uncontrollably ending up on the floor — what was happening to me?

Looking back as I stood there during that time of ministry, I knew that I had been prepared for this. God's word had been confirmed to me as I stood in this Christian women's ministry meeting. The woman pastor called me up front and prophesied to me and said that God was calling me into the Gospel ministry. How did she know? Did God tell her too? She didn't know me or who I was — yet here she was standing before me telling me what God had already revealed to me.

I had been searching for some time...Seeking God in prayer and study. I had even joined a few ladies from another church to have a Bible study, going from house to house. The lesson I remember most was a teaching on the Holy Spirit by Kenneth Copeland that taught who the Holy Spirit was and how He operates in and through us. One evening during the time we were to have our Bible study, we decided to go to a women's meeting in Troy, NY. It was there that I had my first experience and encounter with the infilling of the Holy Spirit. We were asked to come together for prayer by joining hands. The question was then asked if there were persons present who wanted to be filled with the Holy Spirit with the evidence of speaking in tongues. Hesitantly, I raised my hand. I was hesitant because I wasn't sure about what this all meant and how I would be affected. The leader of the group admonished us to begin praying, but not in our English language. As I began praying, the first word that came out of my mouth was "Hallelujah" repeating it over and over again — I didn't know how to speak any other way. What did she mean? Again she said, "Don't speak your normal language, but begin speaking as God gives you the words or utterance". So I forced myself to relax and stop trying so hard. When I did so, some weird words began to flow from my mouth. Things I had never spoken before and could not understand were being said. As I spoke, the strange words were flooding from my mouth — it came quickly and powerfully. The women on each side of me let go of my hands because my arms and hands began jerking wildly back and forth uncontrollably. Euphoria began to overtake me; all self control was gone — a strange power had overtaken me and I was no longer myself. I felt light on my feet feeling a sweet peace. I was high on the Holy Spirit — drunk to the point where if I didn't sit down, I would fall down. New to this, it was hard to understand what was happening. The Holy Spirit had come upon me with so much power — this thing that was happening to me was so amazing. When it was all over, I left feeling so drained, so tired. I had no strength left in my body and went home and fell right into bed.

Sleep came fast and as I slept, I dreamed. In the dream, there was a very large monster. He reminded me of something that I read about in the Bible and had seen on a television program. He had horns on his head, very large teeth and he stood straight up like a human being. There was a large wooden door that was separating the two of us. He was on one side pulling the door, trying to open it to get in as I was on the other side trying to keep him from entering. The dream was so vivid and frightening! Struggling against the pull of this creature, proved hard for me as the monster overcame me and pulled the door wide open. When he did so, a sword and shield suddenly appeared in my hands — the real battle began! As we struggled, I began to yell the words, "In the Name of Jesus! In the Name of Jesus!" Repeating it over and over again! "In the Name of Jesus!" At that point, I woke up still crying "In the Name of Jesus!"

Hebrews 4:12 ~ *For the word of God is quick, and powerful, and sharper than any two-edged sword, piercing even to the dividing asunder of soul and spirit, and of the joints and marrow, and is a discerner of the thoughts and intents of the heart.* I believe it was God's way of telling me that He was calling me to the ministry and that I would have to do battle with my Bible, the Word of God — this was the sword and the shield that was placed into my hands. God had been giving me many signs, preparing me for ministry. There were times He had revealed His purpose and plan for my life as I prayed and spent time with Him in the privacy of my bedroom. As I got more and more into scripture, there were times when He spoke to me through that word. One time as I studied, He vividly spoke to me through Ezekiel 3:4-11 which reads, "*And he said unto me, Son of man, go, get thee unto the house of Israel, and speak with my words unto them. For thou art not sent to a people of a strange speech and of a hard language, but to the house of Israel; Not to many people of a strange speech and of a hard language, whose words thou canst not understand. Surely, had I sent thee to them, they would have hearkened unto thee. But the house of Israel will not hearken unto thee; for they will not hearken unto me: for all the house of Israel are impudent and hardhearted. Behold, I have made thy face strong against their faces, and thy forehead strong against their foreheads. As an adamant harder than flint have I made thy forehead: fear them not, neither be dismayed at their looks, though they be a rebellious house. Moreover he said unto me, Son of man, all my words that I shall speak unto thee receive in thine heart, and hear with thine ears. And go, get thee to them of the captivity, unto the children of thy people, and speak unto them, and tell them, Thus saith the Lord GOD; whether they will hear, or whether they will forbear.*

What does it all mean? Purpose: God's plan for you. He will always in some way, let you know what His desire is for your life. I truly believe in my heart that if you look at the gifts and talents that you have in your personal life and take those things and submit them to God, He will show you your kingdom purpose. According to Psalm 139:13-16, God endowed us with everything we needed to be used for His kingdom even before we were born; purpose takes place in our mother's womb. He has plans for each of us and has already set our days. Look at your life and see how you have affected change in the daily scheme of life — what person or persons have you left an impact on? After you have looked at that scenario, pray and ask God, "How can you use me and this gift or talent so that I can affect change in your kingdom?" My spiritual purpose was clear.

As a child, growing up in a musical family, God's purpose was manifested in me through the music — singing and writing. I first started out just writing lyrics and found this company that could put my lyrics to music. Country music is great for those who are fans of it, but I'm not. The song ended up pure country with a male singer. That was when I made the decision to write my own music. My very first song was titled, "God is Not Through with Me Yet" and was recorded by my group, Odell Wesley Surgick Ensemble. As the years and time went by, I got better and better and started publishing my music. Another song called "Blessed Is the Name" was chosen and was one of the featured songs at the yearly Hampton, Virginia University Ministers Conference/Choir Directors and Organist Guild annual concert. Hampton University was one of the places that my mom and I would travel to every June. Year after year, we would pack up and go for a full week to be in the mix of ministers, musicians, singers and songwriters with a passion to enhance our craft and to hear the gospel preached by mighty men and women of God.

After attending the conference for many years, Dr. Roland Carter, the Director of Music chose my song to be one of the songs to be sung by a 1,400 voice choir at the closing night concert. At this concert, there was a repertoire of hymns, spirituals, anthems and gospels that were rehearsed during the week to be presented; what an honor and privilege...It was one of my greatest moments.

As thousands of people poured into the convention center, I sat in the balcony waiting with great anticipation to hear my song; just giggling and laughing on the inside — waiting for a song that God had blessed me with to be sung by a 1,400 voice choir...Heard by thousands of people in this convention center arena! It was so overwhelming! I was finally being recognized as a legitimate song writer, with people asking me for my autograph! I remember how when the song was introduced, Dr. Carter asked me to stand and how the people applauded me — it was such a great feeling watching the people sing and enjoy a song that God had blessed me to write fulfilling my purpose.

This same song, "Blessed Is the Name" was introduced in the new music seminar at the James Cleveland Gospel Music Workshop of America and was also sung by the Ramsey High School Choir all over Birmingham, Alabama. Since then, God has blessed me to write many songs of praise and worship to Him. I give all glory and honor to God for all the gifting He has placed in me.

Through it all, Satan had it out for me. He tried to stop me from doing and being all that God had created me to be. I am a worshipper; Satan is jealous of anything and anyone that worships the majesty of God. Because of that, it was his prime plan and purpose to do all he could do to hinder me in any way he could to stop me from using the gifts and talents that God has endowed me with to worship the living God, our Creator. Satan tried to stop me by using my sadness and loneliness to take the focus off of my purpose, but through God I was victorious.

MY MESSAGE TO THE READER:

Your purpose will be manifested by God as He uses you for His kingdom's sake. Yes, Satan will use all sorts of tactics to get you out of step with that purpose; but you have to let him know that God is in control and that you will not allow anything to pull you away from that control. Look at your life today and see all of the wonderful things that God has planned for you and then begin to walk in that purpose for the kingdom's sake. Now pray and ask God — He will surely answer you with clarity.

CHAPTER 6

My Earthly Being and Insecurities Being Mastered

I will praise thee; for I am fearfully and wonderfully made: marvelous are thy works; and that my soul knoweth right well. Psalm 139:14

After mom passed away, life began again and I began to pour my heart and soul into ministry at church. I worked in the church office and there were many long hours in that office as I tried my best to keep up with the work load in addition to being the Minister of Music. At that time, I was working there as a secretary. I wasn't very good at the organization and filing, but I sure could handle a keyboard — seventy to seventy-five words a minute. There were times that I could not even finish one job when something that was deemed more important would take precedence over the job I was working on and having to drop everything to get the new job done; I guess that's the way of any productive organization. As I said, I wasn't that good in my organizational skills and many times that would get in the way of having a good working atmosphere. The Pastor would chug out that work like a running freight train barreling through a big town — never ending — never stopping and never looking back. It was really hard trying to keep up with her and most times it was a real detriment to the success I felt in administration. I was already suffering with some childhood issues that had followed me into adulthood — low self esteem — always feeling like a failure — being quiet and shy. There were many times that I was taken back in my mind to my childhood days, as I struggled to get by in the office.

Looking back, I had some very lonely and difficult days as a child. When I was in the fourth or fifth grade, our family moved to Colonie, NY. It was very hard for me, being the only black child in a predominately white school in most of my classes. Some of the kids were very cruel — calling me names, talking about me — not behind my back, but right in my face. They thought my lips were so big that they called me "Ribber Lips". I'm not quite sure who started it or where that name came from, but one day as I walked into school, that's what I was called. Many tears were shed during those dark, lonely times in Colonie.

My childhood was haunted by the taunts of bullies. I'm sure that many children, as well as adults have gone through bullying at some point in their lives; it's all over the news today. Bullying was at its best from some of my classmates when attending that school. Even though I was the oldest of my siblings, there were times when I had to call upon my sister, Denise. She was the bold one and wasn't afraid to get up in your face — even in the face of big white guys who bullied me. I admired the fact that she wasn't afraid. She would get up in your face with no fear while I stood on the sideline, head bowed low with tears in my eyes. Years later taking Karate, she received a brown belt.

When I think back upon my life, my insecurity had not just begun in Colonie, NY, but I can remember some hard times as a child in Albany at school #22 when we lived at 242 Second Street, a house that has now been demolished. The school was within walking distance of our home. Kids bullied me there too. One time I was even spit on in this predominately black school by a white boy and even had stones thrown at me! There were even teachers that were cruel to me. One teacher in particular, Mrs. A---, was trying to instruct us on how to tell time on one of those cardboard clocks with the little metal hands that you can manually move around on the board. She called me up to the blackboard and I stood there having a hard time understanding the concept of time. Because of this, she took my head and pushed it up against the blackboard onto the cardboard clock. In doing so, she broke my eyeglasses. I never told my mom about that until I was an adult. I know that she would have been up in that teacher's face had she known; I really don't know why I didn't tell her — I guess it was all a part of my insecurity in not being able to speak up. It was as if my insecurity really caused me to walk around with an imaginary sign on my back that said, "pick on me and get away with it."

In Colonie, NY, I'll never forget another teacher, Mrs. M---. I despised that woman. She always had a scowl on her face; black hair pinned up in a big bun on the top of her head with an angry, military type of spirit all over her. She was so mean and hurtful to me. I remember one time we were studying an English lesson and she asked me to read a paragraph which she had written on the blackboard. The first line she wrote on the chalkboard ended with "Is" followed by a hyphen. On the next line, the sentence began with the word "land". So naturally, from a child's point of view I began reading it, as "Is… land". This woman went ballistic; I would equate her demeanor as being one most like a temper tantrum or a boiling pot that spilled over, yelling at me — and of course, me being who I was at that time, began to cry. Seeing my tears, she told me to leave the classroom and go stand out in the hallway — embarrassing me in front of a room full of white kids! It actually made me hate her all the more. On days that she was late getting into the classroom, I would privately wish that she was sick and wouldn't show up. One day I wished it and she didn't show up because she was sick. How happy I was!!

In my mind, I really didn't have a childhood like most other children. I had a problem with socializing and didn't have very many friends at all while growing up. But, there was one girl I will never forget. She was a real friend to me and helped me to get through a lot of painful, lonely days and years in the Colonie School District

— Jeanette Hebbard was her name. Even though she was white, she didn't let that stop her from being a real friend to me and this other girl, who was mentally challenged, named Roberta. I was even invited to her home for lunch on several occasions and I was welcomed warmly into that home by her mother. She was a true friend to me. It's funny, but I was going to ask her to be in my wedding, but coincidentally she couldn't because she was getting married the very same day that I was — August 25, 1973. I lost track of Jeanette and often think about her and wonder where she is today — wanting to find her and thank her. She was the only one that I could really call a friend those lonely high school days.

With the exception of Jeanette, I've really never had anyone that I can really call a true friend other than my mom. When I think of a friend, I'm looking for someone I can hang with — go out and see a movie, go to lunch, go shopping, sit around and talk, go for a walk, exercise together. Life is funny when it comes to relationships; there are friends you will have for a lifetime, friends that you don't often speak to but know that they are always there when you need them and there are friends that will only be with you for a season. Penned by Eleanor Roosevelt, this quote speaks volumes, "Many people will walk in and out of your life, but only true friends will leave footprints in your heart". This is a true saying that can mean so much to a good relationship.

When I look back, it is apparent that my shyness got in the way of having good friend relationships. You've heard the quote, "to acquire friends, show yourself friendly' or as Ralph Waldo Emerson put it, "The only way to have a friend is to first be one". I may be wrong but I really believe that shyness was the detriment to my having any meaningful friendships. Because of this, I have spent many lonely days and nights hungering for a friend. I once had a friend at my childhood church that truly met my definition of being a friend. We did the things that friends do; we shopped, would go to lunch and celebrate each other's birthday by going out to dinner. We did this for years, but a church issue turned things upside down. The church I grew up in, split and while I left that congregation, she remained there. Right after the split, in a telephone conversation, I asked her if my leaving was going to affect our friendship and she said, "We'll have to talk about that". A true friend would not let anything get in the way of a real relationship and when she made that statement, she all but told me that she was not a real friend and that the relationship split just as the church had split.

I believe that my friend issue caused a domino effect of very negative thinking in my life. In order to make friends, I had based my life on trying to be a people pleaser. I was easily attracted to a friendly person and always wanted to be noticed by others; "See me! Do you see me?" That's really what my life was like before I finally grew up and matured in my thinking. I grew up in relationship with God finally realizing that the only person I needed to impress was Him alone. He is the real, true friend that I've never had. I had to make the choice to be my own authentic self and live for Him and not for man. When I accepted Christ as my personal Savior and grew up in this knowledge, people were left in shock not understanding what had taken place in my life and how God had changed me. This radical change left them wondering and asking the question, "What has happened to Theresa?" No longer was I an adult, acting like the child I once was who walked with her head hanging low, watching the cracks and lines in the concrete of a sidewalk; no longer was I afraid to speak in public, fearful of people and their opinion of me — but I could now stand proud with my head held high and speak fearlessly to anyone who would listen. I had to make the choice to live life! I could no longer let people walk all over me with their hurtful and degrading words — words that were an untrue attack on my character. I could have been like so many people in the world who have literally lost the will to ever achieve anything in life because of degrading, hurtful, unmerited words. I knew that there was so much more to my life that God had purposed for me and I had to make the choice to shake off that spirit of low-self esteem and live the life that was purposed especially for me by God.

In coming to this realization, I had to leave behind a lot heavy baggage — stuff that had worn me down. Insecurity, fear of failure, feeling ugly, inadequate and lonely as well as being made to feel stupid — this is heavy baggage that you have to put down, step back and see yourself as God sees you! I soon came to the realization that many times, man will put you down because he is envious or he sees something in you that he wishes he had. I had to realize that God loves me and has made me in His image — therefore, in the eyes of God, I am perfect.

MY MESSAGE TO THE READER:

My friend, you have to face that enemy of degradation and boldly tell him that you will no longer be controlled by him — go head to head with him and make the choice to live a life of freedom and love in Christ. It's time to leave the baggage where it belongs — in the garbage and pick up all that God desires for your life. You can do it and will do it if you make the choice to let the fear go. It has trampled you down long enough! You are not by yourself....The Spirit of God is with you to lead and guide you. With His help, strength and power, you can and will leave that old baggage behind and live an abundant life!!

CHAPTER 7

My Focus Error

The statutes of the LORD are right, rejoicing the heart; the commandment of the LORD is pure, enlightening the eyes. Psalms 19:8

I had not yet conceived it, but in my prayer time God was trying to give me a revelation. He had brought a word to me that was very hard for me to receive — He told me that I had personally placed myself in a type of exile. This exile was caused through my own desire to be loved and to please men. This exile was caused because of my own lustful desires — it was a man made exile. "Exile" is the state or a period of forced absence or a period of voluntary absence from your country or home. Clearly, I was in exile! I placed myself there voluntarily because I was looking for something more than what I felt I was getting. I had alienated myself from my family, from my old church acquaintances and friends — all because I was looking for some love and acceptance trying to replace the relationship that I had lost with the sickness and eventual death of my mother. I was looking for someone to take me away from all of the pain that I was feeling at that time — rejection, grief and loss. My mother, being sick and then losing her in death had taken a great toll on me. I couldn't handle it by myself and because I was feeling so depressed and was in such a vulnerable state, I was drawn away by my flesh and saw something that I thought resembled God. I was hooked and drawn in by man's charismatic words. I became a man pleaser and not a God pleaser.

Galatians 1:10 — "Am I now trying to win the approval of human beings, or of God? Or am I trying to please people? If I were still trying to please people, I would not be a servant of Christ."

The void left in losing my mother caused me to act irrationally. Spiritually, I was dead and God was nowhere in this journey. Sometimes staying where you are spiritually is actually moving back-wards. What was good then may not be good for you now.

I was in a ministry that had been a true blessing for me. In the beginning of my time there, it was a new thing for me and I learned so much as God was moving me into areas and places that I had never heard of or even knew existed; He used me and grew me up through word, song and prayer. But now, God was no longer in this; it was about my personal issues and pleasing man — trying to replace lost love; trying to make sure I did everything right in man's eyes so I would be loved and patted on the back for doing a good job; trying to say all the right words at the right time — trying not to stir up anything that could be stirred. I did things out of obligation to man and not to God so that man would love me. I was fearful of what would happen or what would be said if I didn't do something right or with any inkling of imperfection. What would happen? Would I be criticized in front of others? Would there be some kind of tongue lashing? I don't know, but I was afraid that at any moment, I would be called out for my ineffectiveness and that love that I was feeling would be lost once again, stirring up failure and defeat. Because of this, I ended up being spiritually and emotionally depleted and on edge with feelings of this failure that permeated my whole being. In addition to all of this, I was physically and mentally burned out. I was in a place of pain and didn't know how to move from that pain. Often when you are in a place of pain, you protect that pain by con-fining yourself, placing a moat around your heart with one way in and one way out... like a drawbridge, a controlled environment — you can see what is coming and going, you know what to expect and thereby reduce the potential of anyone ever touching that sore place even if the touch is to heal.

I was trying to think myself happy, but it wasn't working. The Bible says, "As a man thinks, so is he" — but thinking and trying to make myself happy just wasn't working for me at the time. If the truth be told, I had become a puppet in the kingdom of God and the church was my puppet master. I was being controlled by man — waiting for him to push my buttons or pull my strings showing me the next direction to take. It was a very unhealthy situation, but I couldn't see it because I was totally immersed in it. I had gone through so much for so many years; bouts of depression, sadness, anger and feelings of failure, hurt and emptiness that had dug deep into my spirit — it was something that I had tried hiding for a long time, going about my business and wearing a smiley mask to hide any true feelings.

Now, I was desperate to get away — It was time for me to leave the ministry. I was so tired and stressed out. I tried taking myself down from leadership a few times but was always pulled right back into it by upper leadership. I loved the pastors but thoughts of getting onto a bus and going somewhere — anywhere, just to get away from it all had crossed my mind many times. I was even trying to convince my husband to move us to another city out of fear that if we left that church and went to another church within the city, I would have to put up with the repercussions — the aftermath and the shame.

It was time... there was a giant crack in the road that prevented me from moving any further and I felt like I was stuck with no way of crossing over to get away to the other side. It was time for me to grow up and face reality — I could either stay there and be miserable or find a way to make it across to my destiny in becoming a truly mature, healed woman of God. It was time for me to leave the nest. I was grown and the feelings that I once had when I was in a childlike state in need of strong parents just to survive day to day were now gone. When you mature and begin to heal, you put away childish things, make strong decisions on behalf of your family, and operate in sincerity and oneness with God rather than oneness with man. It became apparent that I had to leave the house to be the woman God called me to be. My role was now set by God.

The decisive point in my journey came in the form of a situation with my daughter. I had to break the confidence of the one who shared it with me. I broke and addressed it head-on. It was here that a line had to be drawn for the boundaries of influence over the affairs of my family. The love for my daughter woke me up, shook me to the core. In this situation, I had to stand up and be a real woman- -- for myself and my family. The result was catastrophic. I isolated my pastor, who wanted to present a strong unified message to my daughter about what she was going through. In doing so, I also isolated my husband and my daughter. So we left the place of worship where we all had built a spiritual foundation.

Even before this situation came about, something had died inside of me. I had gotten to the point where I was now forcing myself to go to church, finding any excuse for not going and only went out of obligation and thinking that if I didn't attend, I would probably get in trouble. I was walking in fear...Feeling out of place. For years, I had taken the path of least resistance. Instead of taking action, I gave in not wanting to cause any confusion or trouble for anyone. So I stayed. When you take the path of least resistance, you never want to find yourself in direct confrontation with a formidable problem — you just roll with the die and control situations with non-confrontational actions. Most people can change the situation by taking the path of least resistance, but for me, because I was filled with fear of the outcome, I stayed and did what I had to do to get by just to survive. Desperation puts you in survival mode.

My season in this place of worship had come and gone. So after years of living this way, I gained enough boldness to leave it behind. After much prayer and going back and forth with my feelings and a battle in my mind, I got the boldness to write a letter to the pastors:

August 10, 2009

To Pastors:

To the Leadership Board:

It is with a very heavy and sad heart that I submit my resignation from Leadership and my departure from the fellowship. I believe that my season has ended. Again, I apologize for all of the trouble I have caused you and the others that it has affected — I sincerely apologize for the hurt that I have especially caused you. Because you hurt, I hurt and because of this, I have not been able to move beyond the pain of it all. It has caused me not to be present spiritually when I am there. I feel like I am disjointed and have been very unhappy, have no joy and have really struggled even to go to church. It has been so hard for me to even walk into church. I have no one to blame but myself — It's something I'm going through. I need to go somewhere else and just sit for a while. I never thought that wanting to get to the bottom of a trying situation with my child would lead to so much trouble and hurt. I will always love you and will always have nothing but good things to say about you, who will always be my Pastors, and ministry. I will continue to send my tithes and offering until I settle in a place of worship. I love you and will always remember and walk in the teachings I have learned and the many good times that I have enjoyed being a part of this wonderful, God blessed ministry.

With God's Love,

Theresa M. Odom-Surgick

What a ripple effect was on the horizon! Based on what I had written, the events that followed the receipt of this letter were disturbing. Misdiagnosed or undiagnosed pain is a serious disease. When it is not healed, it speaks for itself in others and multiplies itself unbridled, much like cancer cells that riddled the bodies of my loved ones. I believe the following interactions came from a place of pain beyond this already painful situation, that was hard to understand.

I was criticized and was called a coward. The things that were said hurt and have given me so much time to think about all that transpired. Furthermore, my situation was made even more difficult because my supervisor at work was associated with the ministry. She stopped talking to me and was very cold towards me. Things came to a head with us one day when she called me into a meeting in her office. As she spoke to me, there was a hardness in her voice and a coldness in her look — I got so disgusted with her attitude and said to her, "ever since I left the church, you have made it so hard (I think I used the word "hell") for me. You have been cold towards me and not talking to me; you look at me with disgust in your eyes". With that, she got very indignant and started yelling at me and said, "Well since you brought the church up….." I interrupted her and said that I did not want to talk about the church anymore and that we should not bring the church into the workplace. She then proceeded to tell me "shut up, shut up!" I then said, "Don't tell me to shut up" and I stood up to leave. She said, "I'm not finished with you", yelling at the top of her voice — "If you walk out that door, then you pack up your stuff and leave." Not wanting to get fired, I sat down as she continued ranting and raving.

Not being able to take it anymore, and not wanting to be subjected to anymore of her anger towards me, I made the decision to get up and walk out the door. She jumped up and yelled for me to get my stuff and leave. Walking to my office, my heart was pumping so hard and fast; my hands were shaking uncontrollably as I picked up the phone to call my husband, which proved to be unsuccessful. As I put the phone back down in the cradle, she rushed into my office and told me that the Director wanted to see me in his office. I followed her into his office. I went in and he asked me what the problem was and I explained to him the situation and how she was taking my leaving the church personal and had brought it into the workplace. When I was finished with my explanation, I watched as she sat there and tried very hard to convince him to fire me — to let me go with my two weeks pay. Because of God's grace and mercy, the Director had the wisdom not to do so. He spoke to me about how they were trying to make people more accountable for their work — she had convinced him that I was not doing a good job. Now mind you, I had received two Employee of the Quarter awards (2007 and 2008). He then asked me if I was prepared to continue working with her and to do my best at my job. I said, "Yes, I always try to do the best that I can". He then asked her the same question and failing to answer, she persisted with her protesting and trying her best to convince him to fire me. He said, "No, we'll leave it as is for now" and then he asked if he could speak to her alone. I'm not sure what the conversation entailed, but as I walked away from that office, I knew that somehow, someway I had to get away — I would never be entirely free until I was away from her.

I wonder to myself, how and why I stayed with the ministry for so long. One time I remember asking God this question: "Am I supposed to live out the rest of my life feeling this insurmountable pressure...feeling like a failure and not accomplishing anything in life?" I was called a coward for leaving, but in reality, if I was really a coward, I would have left long before this time; but I stayed. What made me stay? I have always been one who is faithful and true to whatever I am involved with and my word is sure. When I say something or make a promise, you can always count on me to keep my word; that's just me. Because of who I am, I had to do whatever I could do to be a faithful member and follower of the ministry and I really loved the pastors with all of my heart. If you said "be there", I was there and on time. If you said "do this"- I would do it. No matter the situation, I had to remain faithful and true. Also, because I am generally a soft spoken person, many people looked at me and took that for weakness; they got the shock of their lives when I actually stood up for myself and left. In doing so, it caused a lot of anger — so much hurt and confusion for many people. You may say, well why? Why did it take so long? And what was the driving element or force that made it happen? At first I couldn't understand it myself — how I could make such a sudden, drastic move. It was a decision that had been haunting and taunting me for a long time....Enough was enough. Life is too short to go day by day, living in stress, being controlled by other people's feelings and emotions, not enjoying the life that God has purposed and planned for your own life. I had lost focus and had put a man in front of God.

In digital photography, a FOCUS ERROR is an aberration of the auto focus — meaning the camera focuses on a subject but the lens is not aligned correctly, causing a blurred image. I had a focus error in my life; an aberration that had caused me to not be aligned correctly with the things of God, causing a blurry image of what I saw and what God was seeking for my life. I was out of sync with the will of God. I was performing on my own — out of the will of God. My own personal definition of an Aberration, coming from the dictionary of Theresa is: Aberration is unsoundness or a disorder of the mind due to a small change of an apparent position in your life — which is due to the combined effect of the motion, the twists and the uncertain turn that your life has taken. I had clearly lost focus of my true purpose which God had planned for me because I was grieving — I was grieving because of the loss of my mom — first physically because she was sick and then to death. I was lonely — my only true friend was gone. I let the grief and loss of my mom get in the way of my relationship with God. My response was to give up everything that God had invested in me and because of that, as I said previously, it took me to my own personal exile. My mind was lost in a cloud of depression and weighted down with the cares of this world. Mom was gone so in my sadness, I unconsciously began looking for a replacement — anyone or anything that could take away the pain and love me as she did. And I had found it in a person — and in a ministry.

I truly believe in my heart that it was God that turned things around and prompted me to leave, although I was told that "the devil made me do it." God orchestrated and caused a whirlwind of situations that made me finally open my eyes, sit back and take a good look at what was happening around me, and showing me what I needed to do. I was forced to face reality — God's reality; I had to really take a look at what was real. In the spirit, God took me by my shoulders and shook me up to bring me back to HIS reality.

There was so much that He had for me to do and because of the way things were heading, He set things in divine order for me to leave. My season in that ministry had expired. It was time for me to leave so that I could do His bidding and not be affected or infected by man and his wants and to go to the next level in a ministry that He had personally preordained for my life. God had to pull me out by my shoulders to bring me to my senses. Even when I was free from that place, I was still being controlled by what I could and could not say — receiving disturbing telephone calls — not able to express my real emotions that I really needed to get out in order to heal from years of stress and anxiety. I took myself to that exile and didn't even know that I was doing so.

What are the results of being in exile? The main thing is that it takes you out of the will of God. Before going into exile, there were things that I had been doing that were pleasing to God. Freely singing and bringing people together to sing His praise while watching as people came for prayer and deliverance in the monthly meetings that we had. In a sense, I dismissed all of that never thinking how important it was for those that came to hear the word and song and never taking a look back to see the loss in my doing so. All of this took place because I was in a vulnerable place in life, searching for a human to heal and love my pain away. My flesh had taken control. Everything that was happening around me was all out of kilter; I felt like giving up — giving up all that I had learned and felt in God. Satan took that and made it alive and big within me, drawing me away with the charismatic words of man and dismissing all that God had built and nurtured in me — everything that had been in me since my childhood was lost — the music, the love, the song, the family. When mom died, everything took a back seat; I turned away from it all and didn't give a second look back. I didn't even think about it and how it was affecting others, but most of all, how it would affect my life.

In my exile, Satan made me think that I was no longer good enough or good at the things that I used to do — the teaching of music, the setting up programs — in some way I was made to feel inferior and no more viable — It was definitely time to leave. When I made the choice to let go and let God take control of my feelings, hurts and pains, He showed me the course of action He needed for me to follow in order to be all that He wanted and needed for me to be. I had to pray and believe that God had everything in control. I had to continue being who I am and not let people dictate who I should be and what I should do by acting the way that they did towards me. I had to stay true to myself. This is especially befitting of the job that I had. My supervisor, as I said previously, was a part of the ministry that I left. Out of hurt, she had stopped speaking to me and even though she did so, I made sure that I spoke to her each time I saw her. What a trying time! I actually would pray for her asking God to give her the desires of her heart and to change her — to take away the coldness — to take away the hurt and bitterness that she was feeling. But, there were some days that were very stressful for me. Feeling that I could no longer take the rejection I would pray, "Dear God, either move her to another place or move me — I can't take it anymore, so Father God, please take this away from me. Something has got to give; and it did. God answered my prayer.

On one particular day, I didn't feel like putting up with the stress of the job and my supervisor, so needing to take a mental health day, I stayed home from work. That morning I received a call in which I was told that she had been fired. Although the caller said she was not trying to make me feel bad, it was quite unsettling as she told me that the firing took place because "my supervisor wouldn't fire me". At first I was upset when this statement was made, but after thinking about it, if the Director really wanted me fired, he would have done so himself. There was something more to her being fired than what I was made privy to. At first, with some convincing, I was going to just quit the job, believing that I would ultimately also be fired. But with prayer and encouragement from my new Pastor, I decided to wait it out. I had settled in my mind that I would go into work each and every day with the mindset that any day could be my day to be dismissed. In having this mindset, it would help me not to be too upset when and if it did happen. Even though I know that this was an answered prayer from God, I had gotten so caught up in the situation and feelings of condemnation and guilt made me fail to give thanks to God. I kept thinking about what I was told, "Is it true? Was it all because of me?" I had to come to grips about everything! So what if it was true? God answered my prayer — His time and in His way; as my pastor had said, "I had to get this girl out of my head and just give God thanks for what He had done". After thinking about it and asking God to help me and forgive me for my ungratefulness, I was able to give Him the praise that He so deserved for this answered prayer. He had answered my prayer and the prayers of other prayer warriors who knew of the situation and were in prayer for me. God had moved in this situation.

The next day when I got to work, I got so much support from my co-workers who admitted that they were not surprised that this had finally happened. They were just surprised that it took so long to take place. Now, even though there was a lot more work for me to do having to temporarily take over her job, my regular job and also be a receptionist two evenings a week — the stress was now gone. I could breathe and not feel nervous or afraid of what she would say to me next. How could this not be God who removed this burden and destroyed this yoke? I was at least now able to be happy about the situation without feeling the guilt that was trying to take hold of me.

I was free — totally free from the controlling spirit I had felt for so long. No matter what would be said about me to others, I did not have to put up with the stress any longer. After some time in that position, I was moved into another department in the company and now, I no longer have to work the night shift two days a week! I'm a day worker! I now have my passion back for all that God had invested and purposed and planned for my life. The song was back in my life!

MY MESSAGE TO THE READER:

Focus has to do with your eyes and what you see. Life is filled with various situations — good and bad. Like a camera, each one has to be handled according to what is required in order to bring about a clear view or viable solution. As they happen, don't lose focus of who you are and whose you are. God is there to fight every battle and to help you to get through every trying time in your life. God has a purpose for your life that He wants fulfilled. So as you keep your focus on God and off of what man thinks you should do, you will be victorious. Don't let man cause you to stumble. Seek God and all things will fall into place according to His desired will for your life.

CHAPTER 8

My Restoration Has Finally Come!!

*And I will restore to you the years that the locust hath
eaten, the cankerworm, and the caterpillar, and the
Palmerworm, my great army which I sent among you. And
ye shall eat in plenty, and be satisfied, and praise the name
of the Lord your God that hath dealt wondrously with you:
and my people shall never be ashamed. Joel 2:25-26*

Sometimes God will put you in a situation that will cause you to
stop, forcing you to take a look at what you are doing. It causes you
to look at how you are living, where are you going and how it is
affecting your life and those around you. Even though I was doing
what I thought was right — and the optimal word here is "I" — for
"I" thought "I" was doing the right thing, but because of my circumstances, "I" really was not in the right frame of mind to make
that kind of decision. Because of this, I missed out on so much — I
missed the mark and lost time on my path to where God was taking
me on my journey to His purpose and plan for my life. Although I
have fully addressed the challenges, there were some very good
things that happened in this tested life of mine. Through each, I have
grown so much, learned so much and now, things that were placed
on hold have come back to the forefront of my life. Being used in the

ministry helped me to grow as a preacher and as a teacher of adults and youth and also a creative gift that I was blessed with, came back to the surface from my former Mount Olive Baptist church days — "drama". Just like I write music and lyrics, God blessed me to write plays and skits. I must acknowledge my former pastor for stirring up and restoring this gift. Years before when I was a young adult in my home church, I along with a friend at church rewrote the familiar musical play "The Wiz". James Chambers and I changed the story line — still having the main characters as in the original score, but took it to another level by equating it to one's Christian's journey.

I also wrote my very first full length play called "The Gift". It is a very powerful play about a mother and child who are struggling to make it because their lifeline — the husband and father of the family abandoned them and has been drawn away by feelings of inadequacy, falling hostage to the demon of drinking. It's a story of victory as the family is revived and their faith is renewed. It's a play that will make you laugh, cry and think. The first time it was performed, many people came up for prayer. This was so touching for me because it was an answer to my prayer. The final outcome for me in performing this play was to see that the message of salvation and deliverance would come through loud and clear — and it did. I thank God for the gifts He alone has given to me.

I also started a new ministry — DMO (Delila Melrose Odom) Music and Creative Arts — named after my mom. My mom loved all forms of music and did all that she could to make music a beautiful experience for the church and for her family. If there was a need, Delila Odom would do her best to meet that need. If she had to purchase an organ or a piano — she would do so; microphones, drum machines, speakers, you name it — she would make sure it was there — all for the sake of having a good music program in the church. Outside of church, she also had a loving heart for people who were in need. I remember in one situation, she took this young teen mother and made sure that she and her precious baby had everything they needed to survive. Nothing was too outside of the box for mom. Therefore, I have dedicated this mission to my mom.

Our goal and vision statement is:

"To use our God-given talents to worship the living God, and to inspire others to worship Him through creative expression. We will do so by using our gifts and talents as it pertains to presenting all forms of Christian music, choirs, praise teams, drama, liturgical dance, mime and our skills as musicians. We will glorify our Lord and Savior, responding to the leading of the Holy Spirit to fulfill God's will and call upon our lives, doing it with a spirit of excellence. We will minister His word through singing or playing music, expressive movement, drama and other creative visual art forms. We will partner with other ministries, organizations and outreach programs to provide leadership and musical support. We also seek to educate those involved in the ministry through workshops, retreats and community service".

DMO had our first big event on April 23 and 24, 2010 — our first annual music and creative arts symposium. It was such a beautiful experience and very overwhelming to see the response of the people — standing room only at the play, workshops and arts concert! God was truly in the house as we worshipped, learned and praised Him along with being able to see friends that we hadn't seen in a number of years. It was an awesome experience, orchestrated by God! I am so excited and grateful to God for all of the support and love that is shown from my Pastors, friends and especially from my wonderful family.

With this I close and encourage you to never let the plans of man stop you from doing the will of God in your life. You have to be free to be who you are in Christ Jesus alone. Sometimes you have to go through something in order to be made into something of value. Just like a diamond in the rough, it has to go through the fire in order to come out a thing of beauty. Just like a piece of gold that has to be fired so that the dross can be removed from its surface; the waste matter; the impurity; the trivial or inferior things must be removed before the beauty can shine through. In the end, all that really matters is your stand with God. How does He see you? Have you given your all to Him? Have you surrendered totally to the will of God? Are you moving into the things of God as He has purposed and planned for your life? Are you fulfilling God's plan for your life? *Romans 12: 1-2 ~ I beseech you therefore, brethren, by the mercies of God, that you present your bodies a living sacrifice, holy, acceptable to God, which is your reasonable service. And be not conformed to this world, but be transformed by the renewing of your mind, that you may prove what is that good and acceptable and perfect will of God.*

What things have you let get in the way of your being able to take care of God's kingdom work? Is there a focus error in your life? Is your life being tested? In the end, the only thing that really matters is where and how you stand with God. Have you let others control your destiny because you were afraid to take that first step to overcome and get past that obstacle? There is a quote penned by Dr. Martin Luther King, Jr. saying, "Faith is taking the first step even when you don't see the whole staircase." We have to walk by faith and not by sight. We have to take that first awkward step to achieve goals and not look back. Once that first step is taken, you are making some kind of progress even if it is just one little step. Just like babies who are learning to walk, even though we may fall a few times, we have to get up and keep trying until we get it right and can stand up and move without the aid of others and be excited about where that step has taken us. That first step helps you to move forward towards that preordained goal. The first step is the hardest — it may be a little scary at first, but it helps to get the ball rolling, knocks fear out of the way and will help you to see ahead to destiny where passion begins to explode within you. I thank God for the obstacles and my testing's because had it not been so, I would not be where I am today! Thank you father God for those little bumps in the road. Life is short so we have to use the days that God has invested in each one of us to the fullest and in the way that He desires for each one of us to live it out accordingly. May God bless and keep you the rest of your tested life.

MY MESSAGE TO THE READER:

Recently, I was watching Pastor Paula White on television and she was saying "You can do the right thing, but if you do it at the wrong time, you can miss your God moment". She was saying that success has to do with timing — God never misses His moments. She was talking about cycles of time. My mantra today is — "I have come full circle — I will not miss my God moments anymore. I have walked out of the realm of failure and into the arena of success." Today, I am happy to say that I am free! To use the lyrics of a well known song, "I am free, praise the Lord, I'm free. I'm no longer bound, no more chains holding me. My soul is resting, it's just a blessing. Praise the Lord, hallelujah, I'm free". Restoration has finally come!!

A CLOSING NOTE

My prayer for you is that you take my life and use it as a template of what to do and what not to do. Don't let your life be so interrupted that you can't get back on track. Listen for the voice of God and do what He tells you to do. He has so much for you to do! He needs you to help build up His kingdom. Life is too short — time wasted cannot be recycled so use your time wisely — use it for something substantial that you are passionate about; using it for something that will be pleasing in the sight of God and will make you happy. You are here to please God and not man. Let God have His way within you and through you by using the gifts and talents that He alone has invested in you. In this way you will be blessed to be a blessing to others the way God has purposed and planned for your life. Satan will do all that he can to hinder the process, but as long as you keep God and His ultimate goal for you in your mind and eyes view, you can and will make it — let God have His way!!! FOCUS!!!

With God's Love,

Theresa M. Odom-Surgick

Theresa M. Odom-Surgick
DMO Music and Creative Arts — P.O. Box 5926, Albany NY, 12205
http://dmomusicncreativearts.com
(877) 869-9263

ABOUT THE AUTHOR

Theresa Melrose Odom-Surgick was born and raised in Albany, NY in a Christian home to Benjamin Odom and Delila Melrose Jacobs. She began singing the gospel of Christ at a very young age in the family singing group, known as the Odom Singers.

Music ministry began in 1973, when her mother retired as Music Director of the Mt. Olive Baptist Church. She then began to direct the choir and her leadership span was from 1973-1981 at Mt. Olive. From 1979-1985 she was assistant to the Director of the Capital District Community Choir, Prof. Rudolph V. Stinney (now deceased). From 1981-1988, she was the Minister of Music at the Star of Bethlehem, and was then called to the Metropolitan NTM Baptist Church and served as Minister of Music from 1988-1994. From 1995 to August 2009, she was a Leader, Choir Director, Drama Ministry Leader, Sunday School Teacher and served as Leader and Assistant Leader of the praise team at New Covenant Christian Fellowship. In October of 1981, Theresa founded and directed the Odell Wesley Surgick Ensemble. OWS ministered from 1981-1994 and during that time, recorded their first 45-rpm record singing one of Theresa's first compositions, "God Is Not through with Me Yet." Since writing that first song, she has published and recorded many songs of worship.

One of the most memorable moments in her life occurred in 1991 as her song, "Blessed Is the Name," was sung by a 1,400 voice choir at the Hampton University Ministers Conference/Choir Directors and Organist Guild in Hampton, Virginia. It was also introduced at the James Cleveland Gospel Music Workshop of America in a music seminar, along with one of Gospel's top songwriters, Carol Antrom, who wrote "He's Preparing Me" and "Stand Still" sung by Darryl Coley. The Ramsey High School Choir of Birmingham, Alabama also sang this song at their annual Spring Concert.

As an accomplished writer, she has written several plays, which include "The Gift", "Murder at the Reunion", "Jalena's Revelation", "Baal's Revenge", the dramatic presentation of "Born to Die", "Guilty as Charged" and several skits under the title of "The Conference Room", which were used as altar call presentations.

Today her focus is on using the gifts invested in her through singing, songwriting, presenting and writing dramatic plays with DMO Music and Creative Arts. Her heart's desire is to touch the lives of many people through the Word of God creatively, in song and through drama.

On September 17, 1995, she was licensed and ordained as a minister of the Gospel. Today she is an active member, minister and drama ministry leader at Empire Christian Center, where her Pastors are Tre' and Christina Staton.

THE NIGHTINGALE'S SONG

Written for Min. Theresa M. Odom-Surgick
By: Michelle E. Trotman © 8/24/02

She stepped out on the perch that day to sing her favorite song,

Something didn't seem quite right, as she went along.

Deep within there was a feeling of uncertainty,

Yet this nightingale did chirp oh so joyously.

This feeling grew within her as it did before,

Yet, she stood in ministry to usher the Father through hearts door.

Her voice was so magnificent, the lyrics pure and sweet,

It was this nightingale who brought praises to God's feet.

In the presence of many witnesses her spirit was made strong,

They stood as true testaments; delivered through her song.

Their words would grant her courage, she now sang so fearlessly,

With confidence her notes rang out with heaven's melody.

With gracious heart she began to see, each time she stood in praise,

Her Father was so close to her: He graced her with His rays.

Now this precious nightingale, no longer filled with fear

Sang her praise with faithful heart as heaven lent its ear.

WITH SPECIAL THANKS!

Pastors Tre' and Christina Staton along with the leadership board and church family of Empire Christian Center for your support and love.

Pastor/Dr. Rhonda J. Ferguson, my Cousin/Sister for your encouraging words, love and support.

Professor Natalie Johnson, Dr. Shayla Sawyer-Armand, Rebecca Jones, Yvonne Chandler and Yalanda Cannon for taking the time to read and edit.

Mary Jane Photography

Victoria A. Dickson Photography

CPSIA information can be obtained at www.ICGtesting.com
Printed in the USA
BVOW042351060512

289295BV00001B/31/P

Option 2

1. What use was made of the lecture method?

   _____

   _____

2. What advantages of this method were in evidence?

   _____

   What disadvantages?

   _____

3. What was the students' response?

   _____

4. Was storytelling used?

   _____

   a. As the main lesson or in support of the lesson?

   _____

   _____

   b. What purpose was fulfilled in its use?

   _____

   _____

5. Were questions and answers used?

   _____

6. What stood out as to principles of good questioning?

   _____

   _____

7. Was creative drama employed to any extent? If so, to
   what advantage?

   _____

   _____

8. Was role playing employed? If so, to what advantage?

   _____

   _____

9. Was discussion used to any extent? As the main method or as a part of the whole lesson?

_____

10. What values did you see in evidence in the use of discussion?

_____

_____

11. Were any projects used? If so, what?

_____

    a. What was the learning outcome?

_____

_____

12. What expressional activities, if any, did you observe?

_____

_____

13. What visuals were employed?

_____

_____

14. What did you observe were significant values of their use?

_____

_____

15. Were the principles of small groups employed in the lesson at all? If so, in what ways?

_____

_____

16. In reference to the lesson plan, were the aims clearly in view?

_____

_____

    a. Were they achieved? _____

    b. Was the plan followed? _____

17. What was the principal method employed in the teaching session?

_____

_____

18. What suggestions could you offer for improving the teaching of the total lesson?

_____

_____

_____

_____

_____

19. What characteristics more or less typical of the age group were in evidence?

_____

_____

_____

20. What procedures in the class did you notice were employed that were a result of the age-level characteristics?

_____

_____

_____